KINGFISHER
An imprint of Kingfisher Publications Plc
New Penderel House
283–288 High Holborn
London WC1V 7HZ
www.kingfisherpub.com

First published by Kingfisher 2006
2 4 6 8 10 9 7 5 3 1

A CIP catalogue record for this book is
available from the British Library.

ISBN-13: 978 07534 1335 7
ISBN-10: 0 7534 1335 3

Printed in India
1TR/0306/BRIJBS/PICA(PICA)/90WFO/C

OVER
150
SPOOKY
JOKES!

Illustrated by **Martin Chatterton**

KINGFISHER

What is a baby ghost's favourite game?
Peeka-boo.

What's the difference between a deer running away and a small witch?
One's a hunted stag, the other's a stunted hag.

What is a vampire's favourite ice cream flavour?
Veinilla.

Why do witches fly on broomsticks?
Vacuum cleaner cords aren't long enough.

What fairy tale do ghosts like best?
Sleeping Boo-ty.

Why didn't the skeleton cross the road?
He didn't have the guts.

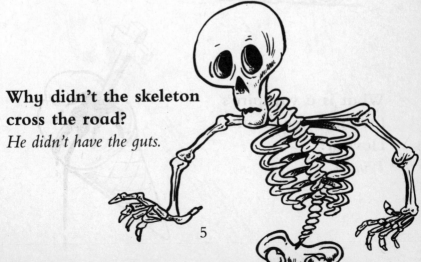

What type of dog do vampires like the best?
Bloodhounds.

Do zombies eat popcorn with their fingers?
No, they eat the fingers separately.

What kinds of ghosts haunt skyscrapers?
High spirits.

What's a monster's favourite bean?
A human bean.

What happened when the little witch was naughty at school?
She was ex-spelled.

What's red, sweet and bites people?
A jampire.

Why do mummies have trouble keeping friends?
They're too wrapped up in themselves.

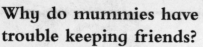

How do ghosts like their eggs cooked?
Terrifried!

What do you call a dead chicken that likes to scare people?
A poultrygeist.

Mummy, Mummy, all the kids call me a werewolf!
Never mind, dear, now go and comb your face.

What goes, "Cackle, cackle, boom!"?
A witch in a minefield.

Why wasn't the vampire working?
He was on a coffin break.

What do skeletons say before eating?
Bone Appetit!

What did one ghost say to the other ghost?
"Do you believe in people?"

What kind of streets do zombies like best?
Dead ends.

Why did the vampire go to the orthodontist?
To improve his bite.

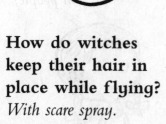

How do witches keep their hair in place while flying?
With scare spray.

11

What did the papa ghost say to his family when driving?
"Fasten your sheet belts."

Why don't skeletons ever go out on the town?
Because they don't have any body to go out with.

What is evil, ugly and goes round and round?
A witch in a revolving door.

What happens when a ghost gets lost in the fog?
He is mist.

How did the glamorous ghoul earn her living?
She was a cover ghoul!

What do you get when you cross a vampire and a snowman?
Frostbite.

What do they teach at witch school?
Spelling.

What did Dracula say when his vampire girlfriend kissed him?
"Ouch."

What did the skeleton say to the bartender?
"I'll have two cokes and a mop."

**What's big and green
and goes, "Oink, oink"?**
Frankenswine.

**What's a vampire's
favourite dance?**
The fangdango.

**What do ghosts
have for dessert?**
Ice scream.

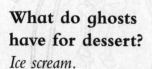

Why did the witch wash her broom?
She wanted a clean sweep.

Who was the famous skeleton detective?
Sherlock Bones.

What do you call a lost monster?
A where-wolf.

Where did the vampire keep his valuables?
In a blood bank.

Why don't mummies go on holidays?
They're afraid they'll relax and unwind.

What kind of spirits serve food on a plane?
Air ghostesses.

What do witches have races on?
Brrrroomsticks!

What happened to the wolf who fell into a washing machine?
He became a wash-and-werewolf.

What is a skeleton's favourite musical instrument?
A trombone.

How does a girl vampire flirt?
She bats her eyes.

Why didn't the witch wear a flat cap?
There was no point in it.

**What does a
skeleton order
at a restaurant?**
Spare ribs.

**What do young
ghouls write their
homework in?**
Exorcise books!

How can you tell if a witch is carrying a timebomb?
You can hear their brooms tick.

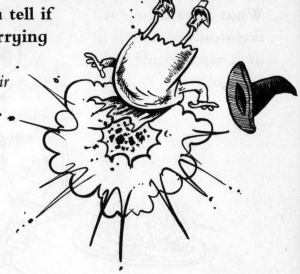

Where does Dracula have lunch?
At the casketeria.

**What kind of ghost
has the best hearing?**
The eeriest!

**Who won the skeleton
beauty contest?**
No body.

**What did the
mummy say to
the detective?**
*"Let's wrap this
case up."*

How did the witches' basketball team do?
They had a spell in the first division.

What is a mummy's favourite type of music?
Wrap!

Why doesn't anybody like Dracula?
He has a bat temper.

What ride do spirits like best at the amusement park?
The rollerghoster.

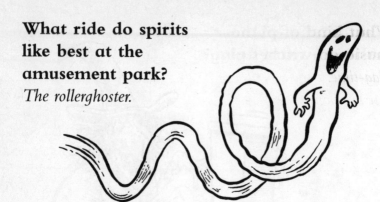

Why did the one-eyed monster have to close his school?
He only had one pupil.

How do you join the Dracula fan club?
Send your name, address and blood group.

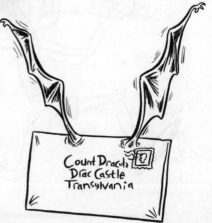

**What kind of piano
music do witches play?**
Hag-time.

**How did the
vampire
marathon go?**
*It finished neck
and neck.*

What kind of pets do ghosts have?
Scaredy cats.

How do you make a witch scratch?
Just take away the W.

Why do skeletons hate winter?
Because the cold goes right through them!

**Why shouldn't you grab
a werewolf by the tail?**
*It might be the werewolf's tail,
but it could be the end of you!*

**Why did the ghost
starch her sheet?**
*So she could scare
everyone stiff.*

Have you heard about the good-weather witch?

She's forecasting sunny spells.

Where does a ghost go on Saturday night?

Anywhere where he can boo-gie.

**Why does Dracula
take art classes?**
He likes to draw blood.

**Why are skeletons
so calm?**
*Nothing gets under
their skin.*

**What was the cold,
evil candle called?**
*The wicked wick of
the North.*

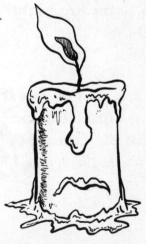

29

Why don't angry witches ride their brooms?
They're afraid of flying off the handle.

What does a ghost have on top of his ice cream sundae?
Whipped scream.

What do you get if you cross Dracula with Sir Lancelot?
A bite in shining armour.

**What do you call
a monster with
no neck?**
*The Lost Neck
Monster.*

**Why are so few
ghosts arrested?**
*It's impossible to pin
anything on them.*

**Why did the
skeleton jump on
a trampoline?**
*To have a rattling
good time!*

31

**Why did the
vampires cancel
their cricket game?**
*They couldn't find
their bats.*

**How do you
get milk from
a witch's cat?**
Steal her saucer!

Ghost: Where do fleas go in winter?
Werewolf: Search me!

What has six legs and flies?
A witch giving her cat a lift.

What did the baby vampire bat say before going to bed?
"Turn on the dark. I'm afraid of the light!"

What do you call a stupid skeleton?
Bonehead.

What does a child monster call his parents?
Mummy and Deady.

What kind of ghosts haunt operating theatres?
Surgical spirits!

Why did the witch celebrate?
She passed her hex-aminations.

What is Dracula's favourite fruit?
A neck-tarine.

What game do ghosts play at parties?
Hide-and-shriek.

What is as sharp as a vampire's fang?
His other fang.

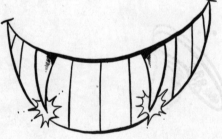

What kind of jewellery do witches wear?
Charm bracelets.

What do you do when fifty zombies surround your house?
Hope it's Halloween.

Where do ghosts post their letters?
At the ghost office.

What do you call a witch who lives at the beach?
A sand-witch.

Why are vampires like false teeth?
They come out at night.

Why do demons and ghouls hang out together?
Because demons are a ghoul's best friend!

Why did the game warden arrest the ghost?
He didn't have a haunting licence.

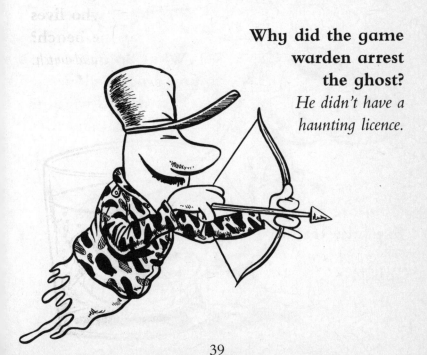

What do you get if you cross a witch with an iceberg?
Cold spells.

What do you get if you cross a dinosaur with a wizard?
Tyrannosaurus Hex.

**Why did the
skeleton stay up
late studying?**
*He was boning up for
his exams.*

**What do young
ghosts call their
mums and dads?**
Transparents.

**What do you call
two witches who
live together?**
Broommates.

What is a vampire's favourite sport?
Casketball.

How do ghosts make a milkshake?
They sneak up behind a glass of milk and yell "Boo!"

What did the mother ghost say to her son?
"Don't spook unless you are spoken to."

Why was the witch kicked out of witching school?
Because she failed spelling.

Why are pixies such messy eaters?
Because they are always goblin their food.

How do you keep a monster from biting his nails?
Give him some screws.

**Why did Dracula
visit the doctor?**
Because of his coffin.

**What is a ghost's
favourite means of
transportation?**
A scareplane.

**Why do vampires
need mouthwash?**
They have bat breath.

Why did the vampire subscribe to the Wall Street Journal?
He heard it had great circulation.

What kind of make-up do ghouls wear?
Mas-scare-a.

What story do little witches like to hear at bedtime?
Ghoul deluxe and the three scares!

Why did the headless horseman go into business?
He wanted to get ahead in life.

Why do girl ghosts go on diets?
So they can keep their ghoulish figures.

What should you say when you meet a ghost?
"How do you boo?"

What is a ghoul's favourite drink?
Lemon and slime.

Where do fashionable ghosts shop for sheets?
At boo-tiques.

Where does Dracula stay when he's in New York?
The Vampire State Building.

Why were ancient Egyptian children confused?
Because their daddies were mummies!

How can you tell a vampire likes baseball?
Every night he turns into a bat.

Who was the most famous French skeleton?
Napoleon Bone-apart.

What kind of music do ghosts prefer?
Spirituals.

What is a vampire's favourite means of transportation?
A blood vessel.

What do you get when you cross a ghost with an owl?
Something that scares people and doesn't give a hoot.

What do you call a wizard from outer space?
A flying sorcerer.

What does a ghoul get when he comes home late for dinner?
The cold shoulder.

Why isn't Dracula invited to many parties?
He's a pain in the neck.

Why are ghosts like newspapers?
Because they appear in sheets.

How do monsters tell their future?
They read their horrorscope.

What did the plumber say when he was called to the vampire's house?
"It's a grave problem."

What is a ghost's favourite party game?
Musical graves.

Who did the ghost invite to his party?
Anyone he could dig up.

What do wizards stop for on motorways?
Witchhikers.

**What keeps
ghouls happy?**
*The knowledge that
every shroud has a
silver lining!*

**Who does
Dracula get
letters from?**
His fang club.

Count Dracula
Castle Drac
Transylvania

**What happened
when the ghosts
went on strike?**
*A skeleton staff
took over.*

STRIKE

What does Dracula drink at breakfast?

Coffin with scream and sugar.

What did the ghost teacher say to her class?

"Watch the board and I'll go through it again!"

What would you get if you crossed a vampire with a snail?
I don't know, but it would slow him down.

Why did the twin witches wear name tags?
So they could tell which witch was which!

What is a ghost's favourite holiday?
April Ghoul's day.

**What airline do
ghouls fly with?**
British Scareways!

**What happened when the
ghost met the zombie?**
It was love at first fright.

**What do little
ghosts wear when
it rains?**
Boo-ts and ghoul-oshes!

**What do you call a
prehistoric ghost?**
A terror-dactyl!

**What is Dracula's
favourite kind
of coffee?**
Decoffinated.

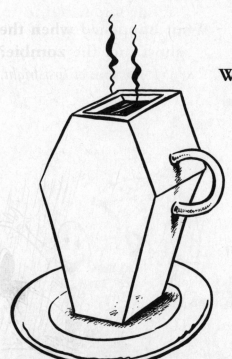

**What kind of jewels
do ghouls wear?**
Tombstones!

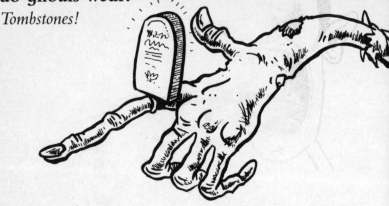

**What happened to the
guy who didn't pay
his exorcist?**
He was repossessed.

**Why can't skeletons
play music in church?**
Because they have no organs.

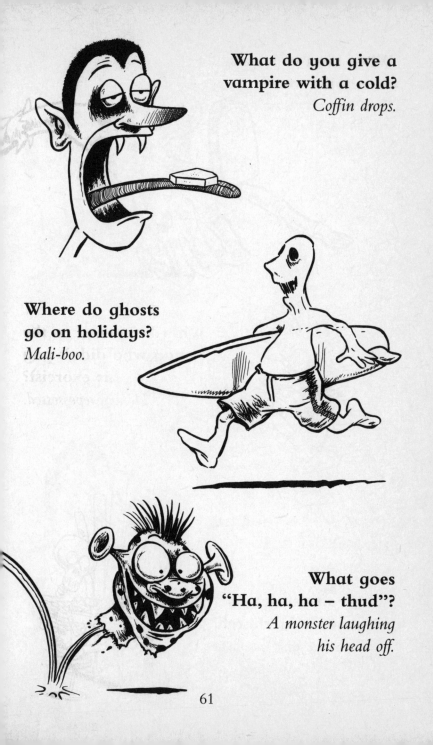

**What do you give a
vampire with a cold?**
Coffin drops.

**Where do ghosts
go on holidays?**
Mali-boo.

**What goes
"Ha, ha, ha – thud"?**
*A monster laughing
his head off.*

**What do you
call a dead cow
that's come
back to life?**
Zombeef.

**Where do
ghosts go
swimming?**
The dead sea.

**What does a vampire
never order at a
restaurant?**
A stake sandwich.

**What do demons
have for breakfast?**
Devilled eggs.

**What trees do
ghouls like best?**
Ceme-trees!